Comparing Autocrats: Analyzing Different Latin American Dictators in the 1950s and 1960s

Comparing Autocrats: Analyzing Different Latin American Dictators in the 1950s and 1960s

By Roberto Miguel Rodriguez

Chapter 1: The 1950s and 1960s: The Age of the Latin American Dictators

The political landscape of Latin America in the 1950s and 1960s

The political landscape of Latin America in the 1950s and 1960s was marked by the rise of authoritarian regimes commonly referred to as dictators. This subchapter aims to explore the intricacies of this era, shedding light on the political strategies, ideologies, and impact of Cold War politics on these dictators. Additionally, it will delve into various aspects such as women's roles, economic policies, opposition movements, human rights violations, cultural expressions, international relations, and the long-term effects of these dictators on contemporary politics and society.

Latin American dictators in the 1950s and 1960s employed diverse political strategies to consolidate their power. Some relied on populism, using charismatic leadership and mass support to legitimize their rule. Others adopted repressive tactics, silencing opposition through censorship, imprisonment, or even violence. These strategies were often intertwined with specific ideologies, ranging from right-wing authoritarianism to left-wing socialism.

Cold War politics played a crucial role in shaping the rise and fall of these dictators. The United States, motivated by its anti-communist stance, supported certain dictators who were seen as bulwarks against Soviet influence. This support often came at the expense of human rights and democratic processes, as the US prioritized stability over democratic governance.

The experiences of women under these dictatorships were diverse. While some regimes sought to modernize and empower women, others reinforced traditional gender roles, limiting their participation in public life. Women became involved in resistance movements, advocating for human rights and democracy, challenging the patriarchal nature of these regimes.

Economic policies under these dictators varied greatly. Some pursued import substitution industrialization, aiming to reduce dependency on foreign goods through domestic industrial development. Others embraced neoliberal policies, opening up their economies to foreign investment. These policies had significant implications for economic growth, inequality, and social welfare.

Opposition movements and resistance against these dictators were widespread, albeit challenging given the repressive nature of these regimes. Students, labor unions, intellectuals, and religious groups played pivotal roles in organizing protests, strikes, and advocating for human rights. Despite facing harsh repression, these movements planted the seeds for future democratic transitions.

Human rights violations and state repression were rampant under these dictatorships. Arbitrary arrests, torture, forced disappearances, and extrajudicial killings were common tactics used to suppress dissent. The long-lasting impact of these human rights violations continues to shape contemporary Latin American politics and society.

Cultural and artistic expressions during this era were both suppressed and subversive. Artists and intellectuals used their work to critique and challenge the dictatorship's oppressive nature, often facing censorship or exile. However, these expressions also served as a form of resistance, fostering a sense of unity and hope among the populace.

International relations and foreign involvement were crucial factors in the survival and downfall of these dictators. The US, as mentioned earlier, played a significant role, but other global powers such as the Soviet Union and European countries also had their interests in Latin

America. These external influences further complicated the political landscape and impacted the trajectory of dictatorial regimes.

The legacy and long-term effects of these dictators on contemporary politics and society are still felt today. While some countries have successfully transitioned to democracy, others continue to grapple with the remnants of authoritarian rule. The political, social, and economic inequalities inherited from these periods continue to shape the region's challenges and opportunities.

In conclusion, this subchapter provides a comprehensive analysis of the political landscape of Latin America in the 1950s and 1960s. It explores the strategies, ideologies, impact of Cold War politics, women's roles, economic policies, opposition movements, human rights violations, cultural expressions, international relations, and long-term effects of these dictators. By understanding this era, historians can gain valuable insights into the complexities of Latin American politics and society.

Historical context and factors contributing to the rise of dictators in Latin America

The 1950s and 1960s witnessed the rise of numerous dictators in Latin America, each with their own unique political strategies, ideologies, and impacts on the region. Understanding the historical context and factors that contributed to their ascent is crucial in comprehending this tumultuous era.

One significant factor that facilitated the rise of dictators in Latin America was the prevailing political instability and economic challenges faced by many countries in the region. In the aftermath of World War II, Latin America experienced a wave of social and political unrest, with economic inequality, corruption, and social grievances becoming pervasive. Exploiting this volatile situation, aspiring dictators emerged, promising stability, economic development, and national unity.

Another critical factor was the influence of Cold War politics. The United States, in its pursuit of containing communism, often supported authoritarian regimes in Latin America, believing they would be reliable allies against the Soviet Union. This led to the installation and maintenance of dictators who were sympathetic to U.S. interests, regardless of their undemocratic practices. This support from the United States not only legitimized their rule but also provided them with economic and military aid, further strengthening their grip on power.

Women's roles and experiences under Latin American dictatorships during this period were also significant. Many dictators enforced traditional gender norms, limiting women's participation in politics and relegating them to domestic roles. However, women played a crucial role in opposition movements and resistance against these dictators, often leading grassroots organizations and advocating for human rights.

Economic policies and development under dictatorial rule varied across the region. While some dictators implemented policies that fueled economic growth and modernization, others prioritized personal enrichment and crony capitalism, exacerbating inequality and impoverishing their nations. The impact of these economic policies extended beyond the dictatorships themselves, leaving a lasting legacy on contemporary Latin American politics and society.

Opposition movements and resistance against dictators were widespread during this era, with student groups, labor unions, and leftist organizations demanding political freedoms and socioeconomic reforms. These movements faced severe repression, as dictators resorted to human rights violations and state-sponsored violence to maintain control. The struggle for democracy and human rights during this period laid the groundwork for future democratic movements in the region.

The legacy and long-term effects of Latin American dictators in the 1950s and 1960s continue to shape contemporary politics and society.

Many countries are still grappling with the consequences of dictatorial rule, including persistent inequality, corruption, and weak democratic institutions. However, these experiences have also sparked a collective memory of resistance and resilience, fueling ongoing movements for social justice and democratic reform.

In conclusion, the rise of dictators in Latin America during the 1950s and 1960s was influenced by a combination of factors, including political instability, Cold War politics, gender dynamics, economic policies, opposition movements, and state repression. Understanding these historical contexts and factors is crucial for historians seeking to analyze and compare the different methods of governance employed by Latin American dictators during this era.

Chapter 2: The Political Strategies and Ideologies of Latin American Dictators in the 1950s and 1960s

The populist approach: Fostering a cult of personality

In the era of Latin American dictators in the 1950s and 1960s, one notable strategy employed by these autocrats was the cultivation of a cult of personality. This populist approach aimed to consolidate power by establishing a strong and charismatic leader who would be revered and idolized by the masses. By creating a cult of personality, dictators were able to exert control, manipulate public opinion, and maintain their grip on power.

These Latin American dictators understood the power of image and charisma. They skillfully crafted their public personas, presenting themselves as saviors and champions of the people. Through carefully orchestrated propaganda campaigns, they projected an image of strength, benevolence, and infallibility. State-controlled media played a crucial role in disseminating this idealized image, with newspapers, radio, and television outlets serving as mouthpieces for the regime.

These leaders often employed a variety of tactics to foster their cults of personality. Mass rallies and public spectacles were organized to showcase the leader's popularity and support. By mobilizing large crowds and orchestrating displays of loyalty, the dictators created an atmosphere of adulation and devotion. They positioned themselves as the embodiment of the nation, claiming to understand the needs and aspirations of the people better than anyone else.

Moreover, these dictators utilized symbols and rituals to further solidify their cults of personality. They designed national flags, anthems, and other patriotic symbols that glorified their rule and emphasized their connection to the nation. Public ceremonies and events were carefully choreographed to reinforce the leader's image as a messianic figure.

The cult of personality was not confined to the public sphere alone. It permeated all aspects of society, including education, the arts, and even religious institutions. Schools were required to teach the dictator's ideology and promote unquestioning loyalty. Artists and intellectuals were expected to produce works that celebrated the leader and his regime, while dissenting voices were silenced or exiled.

However, it is important to note that the cult of personality was not universally embraced. Opposition movements and resistance groups emerged, challenging the dictator's authority and exposing the manipulation behind their public image. These courageous individuals risked their lives to expose the truth and fight for freedom and democracy.

The legacy of the cult of personality in Latin America remains complex. While these dictatorships eventually fell, the impact of their populist approach can still be felt today. It shaped the political landscape, influenced societal norms, and left a lasting imprint on the collective memory of the region. By analyzing the cult of personality, historians can gain valuable insights into the methods of governance employed by these dictators and their enduring effects on contemporary politics and society.

The authoritarian model: Controlling institutions and suppressing opposition

In the tumultuous era of the 1950s and 1960s, Latin America witnessed the rise of numerous dictators, each employing their unique methods to establish and maintain their power. This subchapter delves into the authoritarian model adopted by these leaders, exploring how they controlled institutions and suppressed opposition to consolidate their rule.

One of the key characteristics of the authoritarian model was the manipulation and control of institutions. Latin American dictators skillfully maneuvered their way into power by infiltrating and dominating essential governmental institutions such as the military, judiciary, and legislature. By appointing loyalists to key positions and suppressing dissent within these institutions, they ensured their grip on power remained unchallenged. The centralization of authority allowed dictators to bypass traditional checks and balances, effectively rendering other branches of government subservient to their whims.

Simultaneously, dictators were known for their ruthless suppression of opposition movements. Ruthlessly cracking down on dissent, they curtailed civil liberties, muzzled the press, and imposed strict censorship to control the flow of information. Opposition parties and political opponents were systematically targeted, often facing imprisonment, torture, or forced exile. The authoritarian model relied heavily on fear and intimidation to stifle any potential challenges to their rule.

Furthermore, the dictators' authoritarianism was deeply intertwined with the geopolitical dynamics of the Cold War. As Latin America became a battleground for ideological supremacy between the United States and the Soviet Union, dictators skillfully maneuvered to secure support from one or the other. This external backing often enabled dictators to strengthen their hold on power, as they could rely on military aid, economic assistance, or diplomatic support from their patrons.

However, despite their efforts to control institutions and suppress opposition, the dictators faced resistance from various quarters. Opposition movements, including student groups, labor unions, and leftist organizations, emerged to challenge their autocratic rule. These groups, though often repressed, played a crucial role in exposing the dictators' abuses and advocating for democratic reforms.

Understanding the authoritarian model employed by Latin American dictators in the 1950s and 1960s provides invaluable insight into the dynamics of power during this era. By analyzing their methods of controlling institutions and suppressing opposition, historians can unravel the complex web of factors that contributed to the rise and fall of these autocrats. Moreover, it sheds light on the enduring legacy of these dictators on contemporary politics and society in Latin America, urging us to reflect on the long-lasting effects of authoritarianism on democratic governance and human rights.

The nationalist agenda: Promoting nationalistic policies and anti-imperialism

The nationalist agenda was a prominent feature in the political strategies and ideologies of Latin American dictators in the 1950s and 1960s. These leaders sought to promote nationalistic policies and anti-imperialism as a means of consolidating power and maintaining control over their respective countries. This subchapter will delve into the various aspects of the nationalist agenda and its implications during this tumultuous era.

The rise of nationalism in Latin America can be attributed to a variety of factors, including a backlash against foreign domination and a desire to assert independence and sovereignty. Many dictators capitalized on these sentiments, presenting themselves as champions of the people and defenders of national identity. They promoted policies that prioritized national interests over those of foreign powers, often through the nationalization of key industries and resources.

Anti-imperialism was a central theme of the nationalist agenda, as Latin American dictators sought to challenge the influence of global powers such as the United States. These leaders denounced foreign intervention and sought to establish a more balanced relationship with the international community. They often aligned themselves with other anti-imperialist movements and countries, such as the Non-Aligned Movement and the Soviet Union, in an effort to gain support and leverage against external pressures.

The nationalist agenda also had significant implications for women's roles and experiences under Latin American dictatorships. While these regimes often emphasized traditional gender roles and sought to maintain patriarchal structures, they also mobilized women in support of the nationalist cause. Women were encouraged to participate in nationalist organizations, promote the values of family and nation, and contribute to economic development through their roles as wives and mothers.

Economic policies and development were also shaped by the nationalist agenda. Latin American dictators implemented protectionist measures, such as tariffs and import substitution, to foster domestic industries and reduce reliance on foreign goods. They often prioritized industrialization and infrastructure projects, aiming to enhance national self-sufficiency and promote economic growth.

Opposition movements and resistance against Latin American dictators were also affected by the nationalist agenda. The nationalist rhetoric employed by these regimes often aimed to delegitimize dissent and portray opposition groups as unpatriotic or aligned with foreign interests. This made it challenging for opposition movements to gain traction and organize effectively.

In conclusion, the nationalist agenda played a significant role in shaping the policies and ideologies of Latin American dictators in the 1950s and 1960s. By promoting nationalistic policies and anti-imperialism, these leaders sought to consolidate power, assert independence, and mobilize support. The implications of this agenda were far-reaching, impacting women's roles, economic development, opposition movements, and international relations. Understanding the nationalist agenda is crucial for comprehending the complexities of this era and its long-term effects on contemporary politics and society.

Chapter 3: The Impact of Cold War Politics on the Rise and Fall of Latin American Dictators in the 1950s and 1960s

The United States' influence on Latin American dictatorships

Title: The United States' Influence on Latin American Dictatorships

Introduction:

The influence of the United States on Latin American dictatorships during the 1950s and 1960s was a defining factor in shaping the political landscape of the region. This subchapter delves into the intricate web of relations between the United States and Latin American dictators, highlighting the impact of Cold War politics, economic interests, and foreign involvement. By examining the nature of this relationship, historians gain valuable insights into the dynamics that contributed to the rise, consolidation, and fall of these autocratic regimes.

Cold War Politics and the United States:

The Cold War rivalry between the United States and the Soviet Union played a significant role in shaping the United States' approach to Latin America. The fear of communism led the U.S. to support and sometimes even install dictators who were seen as reliable allies against the spread of Soviet influence. This support often came at the expense of democracy and human rights, as the U.S. prioritized stability over political freedoms.

Economic Interests and Development:

The United States' economic interests in Latin America fueled its support for dictatorial regimes. American corporations sought access to natural resources, cheap labor, and new markets. Dictatorships provided a favorable environment for foreign investment and economic exploitation, allowing U.S. companies to thrive. This economic interdependence between the United States and Latin American dictators further solidified their grip on power.

Human Rights Violations and State Repression:

The United States' support for Latin American dictators meant turning a blind eye to human rights abuses and state repression. The CIA and other U.S. agencies often provided training, funding, and equipment to suppress opposition movements. This collaboration resulted in widespread human rights violations, including torture, disappearances, and extrajudicial killings. The United States' complicity in these violations tarnished its reputation and fueled anti-American sentiments in the region.

Opposition Movements and Resistance:

Despite the United States' support, opposition movements and resistance against Latin American dictators persisted. Civil society organizations, student groups, and political dissidents emerged as powerful forces challenging autocratic rule. Some of these movements received support from international organizations, creating a complex dynamic where the United States found itself on the opposite side of those fighting for democracy and human rights.

Legacy and Long-Term Effects:

The legacy of United States' influence on Latin American dictatorships in the 1950s and 1960s continues to shape contemporary politics and society in the region. The scars of state repression, economic exploitation, and political instability are still felt today. Understanding this legacy is crucial for comprehending the challenges faced by current Latin American democracies and the ongoing struggle for social justice.

Conclusion:

The United States' influence on Latin American dictatorships during the 1950s and 1960s cannot be understated. Cold War politics, economic interests, and foreign involvement all played a significant role in shaping the region's political landscape. By analyzing this complex relationship, historians gain a deeper understanding of the methods of governance employed by different Latin American dictators, the impact on society and culture, and the long-term effects on contemporary politics.

Cold War ideologies and their impact on Latin American politics

Title: Cold War Ideologies and Their Impact on Latin American Politics

Introduction:

The subchapter "Cold War ideologies and their impact on Latin American politics" explores the intricate relationship between the geopolitical context of the Cold War and the rise and fall of Latin American dictators during the 1950s and 1960s. This period witnessed the emergence of several authoritarian regimes across the region, each with its unique political strategies and ideologies. By delving into the historical context and analyzing the repercussions, this subchapter sheds light on the complex interplay between global power dynamics and Latin American politics.

Content:

The subchapter begins by examining the ideological battleground that emerged during the Cold War and how it influenced Latin American politics. It explores the competing ideologies of communism and capitalism, which influenced dictators' strategies and policies to align with one of the superpowers, the United States or the Soviet Union. The subchapter highlights how this ideological divide created a fertile ground for authoritarian regimes, as both sides sought to bolster their influence in Latin America.

Furthermore, it explores the impact of Cold War politics on the rise and fall of Latin American dictators. It delves into how the United States, in its pursuit of containing communism, supported and sometimes even installed authoritarian regimes that aligned with its anti-communist agenda. This subchapter examines key examples such as the United States' involvement in the overthrow of Jacobo Arbenz in Guatemala and the support for the military regime of Augusto Pinochet in Chile.

Additionally, the subchapter analyzes the consequences of these ideological alignments on Latin American societies. It investigates human rights violations and state repression under dictatorial regimes, as well as the role of women and the opposition movements that emerged in response to authoritarianism. It also delves into the economic policies and development strategies implemented by these dictators, exploring their impact on the region's socio-economic landscape.

Furthermore, the subchapter addresses the international relations and foreign involvement in Latin American dictatorships. It examines how the Cold War transformed the region into a geopolitical chessboard, where external powers vied for influence and control. It delves into the United States' interventionist policies and the repercussions of this foreign involvement on Latin American societies.

Conclusion:

By examining the impact of Cold War ideologies on Latin American politics, this subchapter provides historians with a comprehensive understanding of the era of Latin American dictators in the 1950s and 1960s. It emphasizes the complex interplay between global power dynamics, ideological alignments, and the tumultuous political landscape of the region. This analysis contributes to the broader discussion on the long-term effects of Latin American dictatorships and their influence on contemporary politics and society.

Proxy wars and covert operations in Latin America

During the 1950s and 1960s, Latin America became a battleground for proxy wars and covert operations led by global superpowers, primarily the United States and the Soviet Union. These external powers sought to exert their influence on the region, using Latin American dictators as pawns in their geopolitical chess game. This subchapter explores the intricacies of these proxy wars and covert operations, shedding light on their impact on the political, social, and economic landscapes of Latin America during this tumultuous period.

Proxy wars were conflicts fought between two external powers, with local Latin American dictators as their proxies. The United States, for instance, supported dictators such as Rafael Trujillo in the Dominican Republic and Anastasio Somoza in Nicaragua, while the Soviet Union backed leaders like Fidel Castro in Cuba. These dictators, in turn, implemented policies favorable to their respective sponsors, further polarizing the region and deepening the divide between pro-American and pro-Soviet factions.

Covert operations were another tool used by external powers to manipulate Latin American politics. These operations involved clandestine activities such as assassinations, coup d'états, and propaganda campaigns, aimed at either installing or removing dictators sympathetic to their cause. The CIA's involvement in the overthrow of Jacobo Arbenz in Guatemala and the Bay of Pigs invasion in Cuba are notable examples of such covert operations.

The consequences of these proxy wars and covert operations were far-reaching. Latin American societies were ravaged by violence, repression, and political instability. Human rights violations were rampant, as dictators employed brutal tactics to suppress opposition movements and maintain their grip on power. The economic development of the region suffered as resources were diverted towards military expenditures, exacerbating poverty and inequality.

Furthermore, the legacy of these proxy wars and covert operations continues to shape contemporary Latin American politics and society. The scars of state repression and human rights abuses remain, fueling demands for justice and accountability. The region's fragile democracies bear the imprint of this era, with persistent political polarization and distrust in institutions.

Understanding the intricacies of these proxy wars and covert operations is essential for historians studying the 1950s and 1960s in Latin America. It provides crucial insights into the complex dynamics between global superpowers, local dictators, and the consequences for the region. By analyzing these events, historians can shed light on the multifaceted nature of Latin American dictatorships and their lasting impact on politics, society, and culture.

Chapter 4: Women's Roles and Experiences Under Latin American Dictatorships in the 1950s and 1960s

Gender dynamics and expectations under authoritarian rule

In the book "Comparative Autocrats: Analyzing Different Latin American Dictators in the 1950s and 1960s," this subchapter delves into the intricate web of gender dynamics and expectations that prevailed under authoritarian rule in Latin America during the 1950s and 1960s. Addressed to historians, this content aims to shed light on the often overlooked experiences of women and the ways in which gender roles were shaped and reinforced by dictatorial regimes.

Under the political strategies and ideologies of Latin American dictators in this era, traditional gender norms were often perpetuated and reinforced. The dictators, seeking to maintain control and consolidate power, promoted a patriarchal society where women were expected to conform to traditional roles as wives, mothers, and homemakers. These expectations were closely intertwined with the ideologies of the dictators, who viewed women's primary role as supporting the regime and maintaining societal order.

However, it is crucial to note that women's experiences under Latin American dictatorships were not uniform. While some women willingly embraced these gender expectations, others resisted and challenged them. Opposition movements and resistance against Latin American dictators in the 1950s and 1960s often included women who fought for their rights and sought to dismantle the oppressive gender dynamics imposed by the regime.

Despite the gender disparities and restrictions imposed, some women were able to carve out spaces for themselves within the authoritarian system. Women played a crucial role in cultural and artistic expressions during this era, using their creativity as a form of resistance and expression. They used literature, visual arts, and music to challenge the dominant narratives and to convey their experiences of oppression and resistance.

Furthermore, the impact of Cold War politics on the rise and fall of Latin American dictators in the 1950s and 1960s cannot be ignored. The involvement of external forces and foreign powers in these dictatorships often had far-reaching consequences for gender dynamics. The role of women in international relations and foreign involvement in Latin American dictatorships was significant, as they often became victims of human rights violations and state repression, or were used as pawns in geopolitical strategies.

By examining the gender dynamics and expectations under authoritarian rule, this subchapter contributes to a comprehensive understanding of the complex and multifaceted nature of Latin American dictatorships in the 1950s and 1960s. It provides historians with a valuable lens through which to analyze and compare the methods of governance employed by different dictators, as well as the long-term effects of these regimes on contemporary politics and society.

Women's participation in resistance movements

Women's participation in resistance movements during the era of Latin American dictators in the 1950s and 1960s played a crucial role in shaping the political landscape and challenging the oppressive regimes. Despite facing significant barriers and risks, women from all walks of life actively engaged in opposing the dictatorial rule and fighting for their rights.

In many cases, women's involvement in resistance movements was driven by their personal experiences of repression and the desire for a better future for themselves and their families. They played an integral role in organizing grassroots movements, mobilizing communities, and disseminating information about the dictators' abuses. Women's participation was often characterized by their ability to navigate the existing social structures and use their roles as mothers, wives, and daughters to rally support and build networks.

One notable example of women's resistance during this period is the Mothers of the Plaza de Mayo in Argentina. These courageous women, who were mothers of the "disappeared" victims of the military junta, formed a powerful movement demanding justice and accountability. Through their peaceful protests and advocacy, they managed to raise international awareness about the human rights violations taking place in Argentina and put pressure on the regime to address their demands.

Women also played a vital role in armed resistance movements. In countries like Nicaragua, El Salvador, and Guatemala, women joined guerrilla groups and fought alongside men for social justice and equality. They not only participated in combat but also took on leadership roles within these organizations. Their commitment and sacrifice challenged traditional gender roles and paved the way for greater gender equality in post-dictatorship societies.

However, it is important to acknowledge that women faced specific challenges and forms of repression within resistance movements. They often had to contend with patriarchal attitudes and discrimination from male comrades. Additionally, women were subjected to gender-based violence and sexual abuse by state security forces, which aimed to suppress their participation and silence their voices.

Overall, women's participation in resistance movements against Latin American dictators in the 1950s and 1960s left a lasting impact on the region's political and social landscape. Their courage, resilience, and determination contributed to the eventual downfall of many dictatorial regimes and paved the way for greater gender equality and human rights in Latin America. Their stories and contributions deserve recognition and further exploration as part of the broader history of this era.

Repression and violence against women during dictatorships

One of the darkest aspects of Latin American dictatorships in the 1950s and 1960s was the widespread repression and violence against women. This subchapter explores the experiences and challenges faced by women living under the rule of autocrats, shedding light on the gendered dimensions of political oppression during this era.

Under the iron grip of dictators, women's rights and freedoms were severely curtailed. The regimes sought to control every aspect of their lives, enforcing strict gender roles and norms that confined women to the domestic sphere. Women were expected to be obedient wives, dutiful mothers, and loyal supporters of the regime, with limited opportunities for education or employment outside the home.

The dictators used various methods to suppress women's voices and maintain their power. State-controlled media perpetuated traditional gender stereotypes, promoting an idealized image of submissive and docile women. Women's organizations and feminist movements were systematically dismantled, and female activists were silenced through intimidation, imprisonment, and torture.

Violence against women was prevalent during this period, with sexual and gender-based violence being used as a tool of control and punishment. Rape, sexual assault, and forced sterilizations were used as weapons to instill fear and subjugate women. Those who dared to challenge the regime or express dissent were particularly vulnerable to these forms of violence.

It is important to note that women from marginalized communities, such as indigenous women, Afro-Latinas, and rural peasants, faced even greater levels of discrimination and violence. Their intersectional identities made them targets of multiple forms of oppression, compounding their suffering under the dictatorial regimes.

Despite the pervasive repression, women played a crucial role in resistance movements. They organized clandestine networks, provided support to political prisoners, and participated in protests and demonstrations. Women's courage and resilience in the face of state violence and oppression should not be overlooked.

Today, the legacy of repression and violence against women during Latin American dictatorships continues to affect contemporary politics and society. It is essential for historians to examine and analyze these gendered dimensions of authoritarian rule, shedding light on the experiences of women and highlighting the ongoing struggle for gender equality and justice in the region.

By exploring the repression and violence against women during dictatorships, this subchapter contributes to a comprehensive understanding of the complexities and consequences of Latin American autocratic regimes in the 1950s and 1960s. It provides a crucial perspective on the impact of dictatorial rule on gender roles, women's rights, and the long-term struggle for justice and equality.

Chapter 5: Economic Policies and Development Under Latin American Dictatorships in the 1950s and 1960s

Import substitution industrialization and economic nationalism

Import substitution industrialization (ISI) and economic nationalism were key strategies employed by Latin American dictators in the 1950s and 1960s to promote economic growth and reduce dependence on foreign imports. This subchapter will delve into the implementation and impact of these policies, shedding light on the intricate relationship between economic development and political strategies of dictators during this era.

ISI emerged as a response to the prevailing economic conditions in Latin America, characterized by a high reliance on exports of raw materials and a widening trade deficit. Dictators saw ISI as a means to promote domestic industries and reduce imports by imposing high tariffs on foreign goods, providing subsidies to local industries, and implementing strict regulations to protect domestic markets. By doing so, they aimed to create a self-sufficient economy capable of producing goods previously imported, thus stimulating industrialization and fostering economic growth.

Economic nationalism played a crucial role in supporting ISI policies. Dictators emphasized the need to prioritize national interests over foreign influences, promoting a sense of national identity and pride. They sought to control key industries and resources, often nationalizing foreign-owned companies and implementing protectionist measures to shield domestic markets from foreign competition. This was done not only to enhance economic self-reliance but also to consolidate political power and maintain control over the nation's resources.

The impact of ISI and economic nationalism was mixed. While these policies initially led to industrial growth and diversification of the economy, they also had detrimental effects. The heavy reliance on domestic industries often resulted in inefficiencies, as protected industries lacked competitiveness and faced little incentive for innovation. Moreover, the protectionist measures limited consumer choice and led to higher prices for imported goods, adversely affecting the living standards of the population.

Furthermore, ISI policies exacerbated inequality, as the benefits of industrialization were unequally distributed. Wealth and power became concentrated in the hands of a select few, often associated with the ruling elite, reinforcing social divisions and fueling opposition movements.

Overall, the subchapter will analyze the complex interplay between ISI, economic nationalism, and political strategies of Latin American dictators in the 1950s and 1960s. It will examine the motivations behind these policies, their implementation, and their consequences on economic development, social dynamics, and political stability. By understanding these historical dynamics, historians can gain insights into the lasting legacies and long-term effects of these dictators on contemporary politics and society in Latin America.

Economic inequality and social consequences

In Latin America during the 1950s and 1960s, economic inequality was a defining characteristic of the region. The autocratic regimes that ruled during this time period implemented various economic policies and development strategies that exacerbated existing disparities and created new social consequences.

One of the key factors contributing to economic inequality was the concentration of wealth in the hands of a small elite. Latin American dictators, such as Juan Perón in Argentina, Rafael Trujillo in the

Dominican Republic, and Fulgencio Batista in Cuba, maintained close ties with the business and landowning elites. This allowed them to enact policies that favored these groups while neglecting the needs of the majority of the population.

The social consequences of this economic inequality were far-reaching. The majority of Latin Americans faced limited access to education, healthcare, and basic social services. As a result, poverty levels remained high, and social mobility was severely restricted. The lack of economic opportunities and upward mobility led to frustration and resentment among the lower classes, which contributed to the rise of opposition movements and resistance against the dictatorial regimes.

Furthermore, the economic policies implemented by the dictators often focused on industrialization and modernization, which further marginalized rural communities and indigenous populations. Land reforms were scarce, and peasants were forced to work on large estates owned by the elites. This led to the displacement of rural communities and the erosion of traditional ways of life.

The economic inequality also had implications for gender roles and experiences during this time. Women, particularly those from lower socioeconomic backgrounds, faced limited employment opportunities and were often relegated to domestic work. They were disproportionately affected by poverty and lacked access to education and healthcare.

The consequences of economic inequality and social injustice under Latin American dictators in the 1950s and 1960s continue to have a lasting impact on contemporary politics and society in the region. The legacy of these dictators is still felt today, as Latin American countries grapple with the enduring effects of economic inequality and seek to address social disparities through inclusive policies and social programs.

In conclusion, economic inequality during the era of Latin American dictators in the 1950s and 1960s had profound social consequences. The concentration of wealth in the hands of a few elites limited access to education, healthcare, and social services for the majority of the population. This inequality led to frustration and resentment, fueling opposition movements and resistance against the dictatorial regimes. The economic policies implemented by the dictators also marginalized rural communities and had implications for gender roles and experiences. The long-term effects of economic inequality and social injustice continue to shape contemporary politics and society in the region.

Foreign investments and economic dependence

Foreign investments and economic dependence played a significant role in shaping the Latin American dictatorships of the 1950s and 1960s. This subchapter aims to explore the intricate relationship between foreign investments and the economic policies implemented by these autocrats. By examining this aspect, historians can gain a deeper understanding of the impact of external influences on the development, stability, and downfall of Latin American dictatorships.

During this era, many Latin American countries were heavily reliant on foreign investments to fuel their economic growth. Dictators, such as Fulgencio Batista in Cuba, Rafael Trujillo in the Dominican Republic, and Augusto Pinochet in Chile, actively sought foreign investments to finance infrastructure projects, industrialization, and modernization efforts. These investments were often facilitated by partnerships with multinational corporations, primarily from the United States.

One of the primary reasons for this economic dependence was the pursuit of modernization and development. Dictators believed that attracting foreign investments would stimulate economic growth and improve living standards for their citizens. However, this economic model also led to the concentration of wealth in the hands of a few, exacerbating existing social inequalities.

Furthermore, the reliance on foreign investments often resulted in a loss of national sovereignty. Dictators became beholden to the interests of foreign investors, who exerted influence over economic policies and resource allocation. This dynamic created a dangerous imbalance of power, where dictators prioritized the interests of foreign corporations over the needs and aspirations of their own people.

Foreign investments also contributed to the rise of opposition movements and resistance against these dictators. As the negative social and economic consequences of this dependence became evident, various sectors of society, including workers, students, and intellectuals, began to mobilize against the dictatorial regimes. They argued that these foreign investments were perpetuating economic exploitation and undermining national sovereignty.

In conclusion, foreign investments and economic dependence played a pivotal role in shaping the Latin American dictatorships of the 1950s and 1960s. These investments were seen as a means to achieve modernization and economic growth but often led to the concentration of wealth, loss of national sovereignty, and the rise of opposition movements. By examining this aspect of the era, historians can gain valuable insights into the complex dynamics that influenced the governance and ultimate downfall of Latin American dictators.

Chapter 6: Opposition Movements and Resistance Against Latin American Dictators in the 1950s and 1960s

Student movements and intellectual dissent

Student movements and intellectual dissent played a crucial role in challenging the authoritarian rule of Latin American dictators in the 1950s and 1960s. These movements emerged as a response to the oppressive political strategies and ideologies employed by the dictators, as well as the impact of Cold War politics on the region.

In many Latin American countries during this era, students became active participants in political activism, organizing protests, strikes, and demonstrations against the dictatorial regimes. They sought to challenge the suppression of civil liberties, demand greater political freedoms, and advocate for social justice. These movements often drew inspiration from Marxist ideologies, as well as the broader global student movements that were taking place at the time.

Intellectual dissent also played a significant role in opposing the dictators. Scholars, writers, and artists used their platforms to critique the repressive regimes and raise awareness about human rights violations. They produced influential works of literature, journalism, and art that exposed the realities of life under dictatorship and denounced the abuses of power.

However, the student movements and intellectual dissent faced severe repression from the dictators. Many student leaders were arrested, tortured, and even killed for their activism. Intellectuals and artists were often censored, exiled, or silenced by the authoritarian regimes.

Despite the risks, the student movements and intellectual dissent had a lasting impact on the struggle against dictatorship. They helped to create a culture of resistance, fostered a sense of solidarity among the oppressed, and ultimately contributed to the downfall of several Latin American dictators.

Today, the legacy of these movements can still be seen in the ongoing struggles for democracy and human rights in the region. The lessons learned from the student movements and intellectual dissent of the 1950s and 1960s continue to inspire activists and shape contemporary political and social movements.

To fully understand the methods of governance employed by these dictators, it is essential to compare and analyze their different approaches. Each dictator had their own unique political strategies and ideologies, which shaped the trajectory of their rule and the impact on their respective societies. By examining these comparative case studies, historians can gain valuable insights into the dynamics of power, resistance, and social change during this pivotal period in Latin American history.

Labor unions and workers' resistance

Labor unions and workers' resistance played a significant role in challenging the power and authority of Latin American dictators during the 1950s and 1960s. These dictators, such as Juan Perón in Argentina, Getúlio Vargas in Brazil, and Anastasio Somoza in Nicaragua, sought to suppress and control labor movements to maintain their grip on power. However, workers and their unions fought back, utilizing various strategies to resist the oppressive regimes and advocate for their rights.

Labor unions emerged as a formidable force during this era, representing the interests of workers and demanding better wages, improved working conditions, and increased social benefits. These unions played a crucial role in mobilizing workers and organizing strikes, demonstrations, and protests to assert their rights and challenge the dictatorial regimes. In some cases, labor unions even formed alliances with opposition political parties, creating a united front against the dictators.

The dictators responded to this resistance with repression and authoritarian tactics. They often used violence, intimidation, and state-sponsored propaganda to suppress labor movements and maintain control. Workers who were perceived as a threat were targeted, leading to arrests, imprisonment, and even disappearances.

Despite the challenges and risks, labor unions and workers continued their resistance. They formed underground networks, disseminated information, and organized clandestine meetings to discuss strategies and coordinate their actions. This resistance was not confined to a single country but transcended borders, with workers and unions in different Latin American countries exchanging ideas and supporting each other's struggles.

The labor unions and workers' resistance also had a broader impact on the political landscape of the era. Their actions helped to expose the brutality and oppression of the dictatorial regimes, raising awareness both domestically and internationally about the human rights violations and lack of freedoms in Latin America. This increased scrutiny and condemnation from the international community put pressure on the dictators and contributed to their eventual downfall.

In conclusion, labor unions and workers' resistance were instrumental in challenging the authority of Latin American dictators in the 1950s and 1960s. Through their organized efforts, they fought for workers' rights, exposed the abuses of the regimes, and ultimately contributed to the dismantling of these oppressive governments. Their legacy continues to shape labor movements and advocacy for workers' rights in Latin America today.

Guerrilla movements and armed struggle

Guerrilla movements and armed struggle played a significant role in the political landscape of Latin America during the 1950s and 1960s. This subchapter explores the various guerrilla groups that emerged during this era and their impact on the region's dictators.

Latin America witnessed the rise of numerous guerrilla movements seeking to challenge the oppressive regimes that dominated the continent. These movements, characterized by their unconventional warfare tactics and commitment to armed struggle, emerged as a response to the repressive political climate under the rule of Latin American dictators.

One prominent example is the Cuban Revolution led by Fidel Castro, which inspired revolutionary movements across the region. Castro's successful overthrow of the Batista regime in 1959 demonstrated that guerrilla tactics could be an effective method of challenging and toppling dictatorial governments.

Other notable guerrilla movements include the Sandinistas in Nicaragua and the Tupamaros in Uruguay. These groups, influenced by Marxist ideologies and inspired by the Cuban Revolution, sought to establish socialist regimes and promote social justice.

The guerrilla movements faced significant challenges in their fight against dictators. The dictators responded with brutal repression, human rights violations, and state-sponsored violence to suppress these movements. Despite these obstacles, the guerrilla groups persisted, attracting support from marginalized communities and mobilizing resistance against the dictators.

The armed struggle waged by these guerrilla groups had a profound impact on the political strategies and ideologies of Latin American dictators. The threat posed by armed resistance forced dictators to adopt new tactics to maintain their grip on power, often resorting to increased state repression and surveillance.

Furthermore, the involvement of external actors, especially during the Cold War, shaped the dynamics of these guerrilla movements. The United States, fearing the spread of communism, supported dictators in their fight against the guerrilla groups, leading to increased military aid and intervention in the region.

In conclusion, guerrilla movements and armed struggle emerged as powerful tools of resistance against Latin American dictators in the 1950s and 1960s. These movements challenged the dictators' authority, inspired by revolutionary ideologies, and sought to establish more just and equitable societies. The response from the dictators was brutal repression, leading to widespread human rights violations. The legacy of these movements and their impact on contemporary politics and society continues to shape the region to this day.

Chapter 7: Human Rights Violations and State Repression Under Latin American Dictatorships in the 1950s and 1960s

Forced disappearances and political assassinations

Forced disappearances and political assassinations were prevalent during the era of Latin American dictators in the 1950s and 1960s. This subchapter aims to shed light on these disturbing practices, which were used by dictators to maintain control, instill fear, and eliminate perceived threats to their regimes.

Under the rule of Latin American dictators, forced disappearances became a common tactic employed by the state security apparatus. Individuals who were suspected of opposing or challenging the regime would be forcibly taken from their homes, workplaces, or public spaces, never to be seen again. This practice served two purposes: to remove individuals who were seen as a threat and to send a chilling message to anyone who dared to challenge the regime.

Political assassinations were another method utilized by Latin American dictators to eliminate their opponents. These targeted killings were often carried out by state-sponsored death squads or secret police forces. Dissidents, political activists, journalists, and even innocent civilians were among the victims. These brutal acts not only silenced dissent but also created an atmosphere of terror and paranoia within society.

The impact of Cold War politics on the rise and fall of Latin American dictators cannot be ignored. Many of these dictators came to power with the support or tacit approval of the United States, which saw them as a bulwark against the spread of communism. This support often included military aid, training, and intelligence assistance. However, as the Cold War dynamics shifted, so did the stance of the United States towards these dictators. This ultimately led to the downfall of several regimes and the exposure of their human rights abuses.

The forced disappearances and political assassinations carried out under Latin American dictators had a profound and lasting impact on the societies and individuals affected. Families were torn apart, communities were traumatized, and a culture of fear and silence permeated throughout the region. The scars of this era continue to be felt today, as families still search for answers and justice for their loved ones.

By examining the forced disappearances and political assassinations of Latin American dictators in the 1950s and 1960s, historians can gain a deeper understanding of the methods of governance employed by these autocrats. It also serves as a reminder of the importance of safeguarding human rights and the need for vigilance against authoritarian regimes.

Torture and arbitrary detentions

Torture and Arbitrary Detentions under Latin American Dictatorships in the 1950s and 1960s

During the 1950s and 1960s, Latin America witnessed the rise of numerous dictators who employed brutal tactics to maintain their grip on power. Torture and arbitrary detentions became prevalent tools of repression, allowing these autocrats to silence opposition and instill fear within their populations.

Under the rule of Latin American dictators, torture was systematically employed as a means to extract confessions, intimidate dissidents, and crush any form of dissent. Interrogation methods ranged from physical abuse, such as beatings, electrocution, and sexual violence, to psychological torment, including sleep deprivation and sensory deprivation. These brutal practices were often carried out in secret detention centers, where victims were subjected to inhumane conditions and denied basic human rights.

Arbitrary detentions were another hallmark of Latin American dictatorships in this era. Citizens perceived as potential threats to the regime, whether real or imagined, were rounded up and imprisoned without due process or any legal recourse. These detentions were often politically motivated, targeting individuals involved in opposition movements, labor unions, or any form of activism. Families were torn apart, as loved ones disappeared into the labyrinth of dictatorship-controlled detention centers, never to be seen again.

The impact of Cold War politics further exacerbated these human rights violations. The United States, in its pursuit of containing communism, supported and often turned a blind eye to the actions of these dictators, allowing them to act with impunity. This foreign involvement not only provided the dictators with financial and military support but also legitimized their oppressive regimes.

The long-lasting effects of torture and arbitrary detentions are still felt in Latin America today. Survivors and their families continue to seek justice and demand accountability for the atrocities committed during this dark period of history. Civil society organizations and human rights activists tirelessly work to shed light on the past, ensuring that these crimes are not forgotten and that the victims are given a voice.

In conclusion, the use of torture and arbitrary detentions by Latin American dictators in the 1950s and 1960s was a brutal strategy employed to maintain power and suppress opposition. These human rights violations, often supported by foreign powers, left a lasting impact on the region. It is crucial for historians to study and understand this dark chapter in Latin American history to prevent its recurrence and promote a future rooted in justice and respect for human rights.

Censorship and control of the media

Censorship and control of the media were key strategies employed by Latin American dictators in the 1950s and 1960s to maintain their grip on power and suppress dissenting voices. This subchapter examines the various tactics used by these autocrats to manipulate and silence the media, exploring their impact on society and the long-term effects on contemporary politics.

In the era of Latin American dictators, controlling the media was crucial to shaping public opinion and maintaining a favorable image. Autocrats implemented strict censorship laws, often targeting newspapers, radio, and television stations critical of their regimes. Journalists and media professionals who dared to challenge the official narrative faced harassment, imprisonment, and even death. By suppressing free speech and limiting access to information, dictators aimed to control the narrative and prevent the spread of dissent.

The rise of the Cold War further influenced the strategies employed by Latin American dictators. Many of them capitalized on the global ideological conflict, portraying themselves as staunch defenders against communism. They used this pretext to justify the crackdown on media outlets deemed sympathetic to left-wing ideologies. Autocrats also leveraged their relationships with foreign powers, such as the United States, to receive assistance in suppressing dissent and controlling the media landscape.

The impact of media censorship on women and opposition movements was particularly pronounced. Women often faced double oppression, as they not only experienced gender-based discrimination but also had their voices silenced by the dictatorial regimes. Opposition movements, including political parties, labor unions, and student groups, were subjected to severe repression, with many activists forced into exile or underground resistance.

Despite the dictators' efforts to control information flow, some forms of resistance persisted. Underground publications, artistic expressions, and cultural movements emerged as avenues to challenge the autocratic regimes. These acts of defiance allowed dissenters to communicate their grievances, albeit often at great personal risk.

The legacy of media censorship and control under Latin American dictators in the 1950s and 1960s continues to shape contemporary politics and society. The lack of a free press during that period has had enduring consequences on the region's media landscape, with many countries still grappling with issues of press freedom and government control. Understanding the methods employed by these dictators provides valuable insights into the challenges faced by contemporary democracies in the region.

In conclusion, censorship and control of the media were integral components of the governance strategies employed by Latin American dictators in the 1950s and 1960s. These tactics served to suppress dissent, shape public opinion, and maintain the autocrats' grip on power. The long-term effects of media control continue to reverberate in contemporary Latin American politics and society, highlighting the importance of studying this aspect of dictatorship in the region.

Chapter 8: Cultural and Artistic Expressions During the Era of Latin American Dictators in the 1950s and 1960s

Censorship and artistic repression

In the era of Latin American dictators in the 1950s and 1960s, one of the most pervasive tools of control was censorship and artistic repression. These autocrats understood the power of art and culture in shaping public opinion and mobilizing resistance, and thus sought to tightly control and regulate artistic expressions within their regimes.

Censorship was a common practice employed by dictators across the region. They established strict censorship boards and agencies to monitor and control all forms of artistic expression, including literature, music, theater, and visual arts. Anything deemed politically subversive or critical of the regime was banned or heavily censored. Artists and writers were often forced to self-censor their work to avoid persecution or imprisonment.

Artistic repression went beyond censorship and extended to direct persecution of artists and cultural figures who were perceived as threats to the regime. Many artists were targeted, imprisoned, or exiled for their political beliefs or for producing work that challenged the authoritarian rule. This created an atmosphere of fear and self-censorship, where artists had to choose between creating work that complied with the regime's ideology or facing severe consequences.

Despite these restrictions, some artists found ways to resist and express dissent through their work. They utilized symbolism, metaphors, and allegories to convey their messages, often hiding their true intentions behind layers of symbolism and abstraction. This allowed them to communicate with their audiences without directly challenging the regime's authority.

Furthermore, underground artistic movements and resistance networks emerged during this period. These clandestine groups organized secret exhibitions, performances, and readings, providing a platform for artists to showcase their work and reach a like-minded audience. These underground movements became vital spaces for dissent and resistance against the repressive regimes.

The impact of censorship and artistic repression during this time was profound, as it stifled creativity, silenced dissent, and suppressed alternative narratives. It created a cultural void where only state-sanctioned art and propaganda could flourish. However, it also sparked resilience and creativity among artists, who found innovative ways to navigate the oppressive environment and keep the spirit of artistic expression alive.

Understanding the dynamics of censorship and artistic repression during the era of Latin American dictators in the 1950s and 1960s is crucial to comprehending the extent of state control and the challenges faced by artists and cultural figures. By analyzing these repressive practices, historians can gain insights into the complex relationship between power, culture, and resistance in authoritarian regimes, shedding light on the resilience of human creativity and the enduring power of artistic expression.

The role of literature in resistance movements

Throughout history, literature has played a crucial role in resistance movements against oppressive regimes, and the Latin American dictatorships of the 1950s and 1960s were no exception. This subchapter will explore the significance of literature as a tool for resistance in this particular era, shedding light on the ways in which writers and intellectuals used their words to challenge and expose the autocratic governments of the time.

In Latin America, literature became a powerful means of expressing dissent and critiquing the political strategies and ideologies of the dictators. Writers such as Gabriel Garcia Marquez, Mario Vargas Llosa, and Julio Cortázar used their works to unveil the realities of life under oppressive regimes, highlighting the human rights violations, state repression, and economic inequalities that plagued the region. Through their novels, short stories, and poems, these authors captured the experiences and struggles of the people, giving voice to those who were silenced by the dictators.

Furthermore, literature served as a means of preserving cultural and artistic expressions during this dark period. Despite the censorship and control imposed by the dictators, writers and artists managed to create works that defied the oppressive regime. By delving into themes of identity, memory, and resistance, they were able to keep the flame of culture alive, providing a sense of hope and resilience in the face of adversity.

Additionally, literature played a crucial role in building international solidarity and raising awareness about the human rights violations occurring in Latin America. Writers and intellectuals from around the world, such as Pablo Neruda and Jorge Luis Borges, stood in solidarity with their Latin American counterparts, denouncing the atrocities committed by the dictators. Their writings acted as a call to action, urging the international community to take a stand against these oppressive regimes.

Ultimately, the literature of the 1950s and 1960s in Latin America serves as a testament to the power of words in resistance movements. By using their pens as weapons, writers and intellectuals were able to expose the injustices of the dictators, preserve the cultural heritage of their countries, and mobilize international support. Their brave acts of resistance not only left a lasting impact on their societies but also paved the way for future generations to continue the fight for justice and freedom.

Visual arts and music as forms of protest

Visual arts and music played a significant role in expressing dissent and resistance against the oppressive Latin American dictators of the 1950s and 1960s. Through their creativity and artistic expressions, artists and musicians became powerful voices of protest, challenging the autocratic regimes and advocating for change.

In the realm of visual arts, artists employed various techniques and mediums to convey their political messages. Painters, sculptors, and photographers captured the realities of life under dictatorship, depicting the human suffering, repression, and censorship experienced by the population. These artworks not only served as documentation but also as a form of critique against the dictators and their policies.

One prominent example is the Mexican muralist movement, which emerged as a powerful tool for political and social commentary. Artists such as Diego Rivera, David Alfaro Siqueiros, and Rufino Tamayo used murals to depict the struggles of the working class, indigenous people, and marginalized groups. These murals were often displayed in public spaces, making them accessible to a wide audience and spreading awareness about social injustices.

In addition to visual arts, music also played a crucial role in expressing dissent and mobilizing opposition against the dictators. Musicians composed songs that conveyed messages of resistance, hope, and solidarity. They used the power of lyrics and melodies to criticize the authoritarian regimes, denounce human rights abuses, and call for social change.

One example is the Nueva Canción movement, which emerged in Chile and other Latin American countries during this period. Artists such as Violeta Parra, Victor Jara, and Mercedes Sosa used folk music to promote social and political awareness. Their songs addressed issues such as poverty, inequality, and political repression, resonating with audiences and galvanizing activism.

Visual arts and music as forms of protest not only provided a platform for dissent but also contributed to the formation of collective identity and resistance movements. They inspired individuals to question the status quo, unite against oppression, and imagine a better future. Moreover, these artistic expressions transcended national borders, connecting Latin American artists and musicians in a shared struggle against dictatorship.

The legacy of visual arts and music as forms of protest during the era of Latin American dictators continues to resonate in contemporary politics and society. The creative courage displayed by artists and musicians serves as a reminder of the power of artistic expression and its potential to challenge oppressive systems. By exploring the cultural and artistic expressions of this period, we gain a deeper understanding of the complex dynamics between politics, society, and creative resistance.

Chapter 9: International Relations and Foreign Involvement in Latin American Dictatorships in the 1950s and 1960s

United States' foreign policy toward Latin American dictators

United States' foreign policy toward Latin American dictators during the 1950s and 1960s was a complex and often controversial topic. As historians, it is crucial to examine the role that the United States played in shaping the political landscape of Latin America during this time period.

Throughout the 1950s and 1960s, many Latin American countries were ruled by autocratic leaders who used repressive measures to maintain power. The United States, driven by its own geopolitical interests and the context of the Cold War, often supported these dictators, viewing them as a bulwark against communism.

The U.S. foreign policy toward Latin American dictators was characterized by a combination of support, intervention, and sometimes even collaboration. The United States provided economic aid, military assistance, and political support to these dictators, all in the name of anti-communism. For example, in countries like Chile, Argentina, and Guatemala, the United States actively supported military regimes that committed human rights abuses and suppressed opposition movements.

However, it is important to note that not all dictators received the same level of support from the United States. Some autocrats, such as Fidel Castro in Cuba, were seen as threats to U.S. interests and faced direct intervention, including the failed Bay of Pigs invasion in 1961. In other cases, like the Dominican Republic under Rafael Trujillo, the United States maintained a cautious relationship, balancing its support for the dictator with concerns about his excessive brutality.

The United States' foreign policy toward Latin American dictators also had long-term consequences for the region. The support for these autocrats undermined democratic institutions, stifled dissent, and perpetuated socio-economic inequalities. Moreover, the U.S. intervention in Latin America during this era fueled anti-American sentiment and contributed to the rise of nationalist movements across the region.

In conclusion, the United States' foreign policy toward Latin American dictators in the 1950s and 1960s was driven by its own geopolitical interests and the context of the Cold War. While the U.S. viewed these dictators as allies against communism, their support often came at the expense of democracy, human rights, and social justice in the region. As historians, it is crucial to critically analyze the impact of this policy on Latin America and its long-term effects on contemporary politics and society.

Soviet Union and Communist influence in the region

The rise of Latin American dictators in the 1950s and 1960s was not only influenced by domestic factors, but also by the geopolitical dynamics of the Cold War. The Soviet Union, as a global superpower, played a significant role in shaping the political strategies and ideologies of these dictators, as well as in the opposition movements and resistance against their regimes.

The Soviet Union saw Latin America as a potential area for expanding its influence and as a means to counter the United States' sphere of influence in the region. The Soviet Union provided military, economic, and ideological support to various Latin American dictators who were sympathetic to communism or willing to align themselves with the Soviet bloc.

One of the most prominent examples of Soviet influence in the region was Fidel Castro's revolution in Cuba. Castro, with the support of the Soviet Union, overthrew the U.S.-backed dictator Fulgencio Batista in 1959 and established a socialist regime. Cuba became a key ally of the Soviet Union, receiving economic aid and military support, including the deployment of Soviet nuclear missiles during the Cuban Missile Crisis in 1962.

The Soviet Union also supported other communist or left-wing movements in the region, such as the Sandinistas in Nicaragua and the guerrilla groups in Colombia and Peru. These groups often received training, weapons, and financial assistance from the Soviet Union, which further destabilized the region and led to increased repression and human rights violations by the dictators.

However, not all Latin American dictators embraced communism or received Soviet support. Some dictators, such as Rafael Trujillo in the Dominican Republic and Anastasio Somoza in Nicaragua, maintained close ties with the United States and actively suppressed communist movements in their countries. These dictators relied on U.S. military and economic aid to consolidate their power and suppress opposition.

The Soviet Union's influence in the region waned in the late 1960s and 1970s, as the United States implemented a policy of containment and rolled back communist influence in Latin America. However, the legacy of Soviet support for Latin American dictators and communist movements continued to shape the political and social landscape of the region.

In conclusion, the Soviet Union played a significant role in shaping the rise and fall of Latin American dictators in the 1950s and 1960s. Its support for communist movements and sympathetic dictators had a profound impact on the political strategies and ideologies of these dictators, as well as on the opposition movements and resistance against their regimes. The Soviet Union's influence in the region was part of the broader Cold War dynamics, which had lasting effects on contemporary politics and society in Latin America.

Non-aligned countries and diplomatic relations

In the tumultuous era of the 1950s and 1960s, Latin American dictators faced complex challenges in navigating international relations and establishing diplomatic ties with other nations. This subchapter explores the role of non-aligned countries in shaping the diplomatic landscape of Latin America during this period.

Non-aligned countries, also known as the Third World, emerged as a significant force in global politics during the Cold War. These nations, which did not align themselves with either the United States or the Soviet Union, sought to assert their independence and promote a new world order. For Latin American dictators, non-aligned countries provided an avenue to expand their influence and gain international recognition.

One key aspect of diplomatic relations for Latin American dictators was the pursuit of economic benefits. Non-aligned countries presented opportunities for trade and investment, which were crucial for their economic development. Dictators like Juan Perón in Argentina and Fidel Castro in Cuba sought to forge economic alliances with non-aligned countries such as India, Egypt, and Yugoslavia. These alliances allowed them to diversify their economic relationships and reduce their dependence on the United States.

Moreover, non-aligned countries played a pivotal role in supporting Latin American dictators' political strategies and ideologies. Many non-aligned nations shared similar experiences of colonialism and oppression, making them sympathetic to the anti-imperialist rhetoric of Latin American dictators. They provided a platform for these dictators to propagate their ideologies and challenge the dominance of Western powers.

At the same time, the non-aligned movement also posed challenges for Latin American dictators. The movement emphasized principles such as self-determination, democracy, and respect for human rights. This put dictators with authoritarian tendencies under scrutiny, as they faced criticism for their human rights violations and repression of opposition movements.

In conclusion, non-aligned countries played a significant role in shaping diplomatic relations during the era of Latin American dictators in the 1950s and 1960s. These nations offered economic opportunities, ideological support, and a platform for dictators to assert their independence. However, they also posed challenges by advocating for democratic principles and human rights. Understanding the dynamics of non-aligned countries' involvement in Latin American dictatorships is crucial for comprehending the complex web of international relations during this period.

Chapter 10: The Legacy and Long-Term Effects of Latin American Dictators in the 1950s and 1960s on Contemporary Politics and Society

Democratic transitions and the challenges of post-dictatorship societies

The transition from dictatorship to democracy is a tumultuous and complex process, marked by numerous challenges and obstacles. In the case of Latin American dictators in the 1950s and 1960s, the aftermath of their rule presented a unique set of issues that historians must carefully analyze and understand.

One of the primary challenges faced by post-dictatorship societies is the establishment of democratic institutions and practices. Dictatorships often dismantle or weaken democratic institutions during their rule, leaving a void that needs to be filled in the transition period. Historians must examine how these countries rebuilt their political systems, including the drafting of new constitutions, the organization of elections, and the creation of checks and balances to prevent a return to authoritarian rule.

Another key challenge is addressing the human rights violations and state repression that occurred under the dictators. Throughout the 1950s and 1960s, Latin American dictators employed brutal tactics to suppress opposition movements and maintain their grip on power. Historians must explore how societies dealt with the legacy of these violations, including truth commissions, trials, and reparations for victims.

Economic policies and development are also critical aspects to consider in post-dictatorship societies. Dictators often pursued policies that prioritized their personal gain or the interests of a select few, resulting in widespread inequality and economic instability. Historians should examine how these countries transitioned to more inclusive economic systems and sought to address the social and economic disparities left by the dictators.

Additionally, the role of opposition movements and resistance during the dictatorship era cannot be overlooked. Historians must delve into the strategies employed by various groups in challenging the dictators, from student movements to labor unions and guerrilla organizations. Understanding the tactics and goals of these movements is crucial to comprehending the broader context of the post-dictatorship period and its impact on contemporary politics and society.

Lastly, the international dimension cannot be ignored. Cold War politics heavily influenced the rise and fall of Latin American dictators in the 1950s and 1960s, with external powers often supporting or intervening in these countries' affairs. Historians should explore the extent to which foreign involvement shaped the trajectory of these dictators and their legacies, as well as the long-term effects on international relations.

Overall, analyzing the challenges of post-dictatorship societies in Latin America during the 1950s and 1960s provides valuable insights into the complexities of democratic transitions. By understanding the political, economic, social, and international dimensions of this period, historians can shed light on the legacies of these dictators and their lasting effects on contemporary politics and society.

Reconciliation and human rights trials

In the aftermath of the oppressive rule of Latin American dictators in the 1950s and 1960s, the question of justice and reconciliation emerged as a pressing concern. The dictatorial regimes were marked by widespread human rights violations and state repression, leaving behind a trail of suffering and trauma. As historians, it is crucial to explore the efforts made to address these atrocities and the impact of human rights trials on the societies affected by dictatorship.

Reconciliation, in the context of Latin American dictatorships, refers to the process of healing and rebuilding trust within society. It involves acknowledging the past, promoting accountability, and fostering a collective memory that can guide the nation towards a more democratic and inclusive future. Human rights trials played a crucial role in this process.

These trials aimed to bring justice to the victims of human rights abuses and hold the perpetrators accountable for their actions. They provided a platform for survivors to share their testimonies and confront their oppressors in a court of law. The trials also served as a means of documenting the crimes committed during the dictatorships, creating an official record of the atrocities.

The impact of these trials on society was profound. They provided a sense of closure for the victims and their families, validating their experiences and recognizing their suffering. The trials also sent a strong message that impunity would no longer be tolerated, helping to establish a culture of human rights and the rule of law.

However, the process of reconciliation was not without its challenges. Many Latin American societies were deeply divided by the legacy of dictatorship, and the trials often stirred up controversy and resistance. Some argued that these trials were politically motivated or that they risked reopening old wounds without leading to meaningful change.

Nonetheless, reconciliation efforts and human rights trials have played a crucial role in shaping contemporary Latin American politics and society. They have helped lay the groundwork for democratic transitions and have contributed to the establishment of truth commissions and other mechanisms aimed at healing the wounds of the past.

As historians, it is essential to study the impact of reconciliation and human rights trials in the context of Latin American dictatorships. By analyzing these processes, we can gain a deeper understanding of how societies have grappled with their traumatic pasts and how they have worked towards building a more just and inclusive future.

Socio-political changes and ongoing struggles for justice

The era of the 1950s and 1960s in Latin America was marked by the rise of dictators who imposed their rule through force, manipulation, and repression. However, it was also a time of significant socio-political changes and ongoing struggles for justice. This subchapter explores the various aspects of these changes and struggles, shedding light on the complex dynamics of the region during this tumultuous period.

One of the key factors that fueled the socio-political changes was the impact of Cold War politics. Latin American dictators often aligned themselves with either the United States or the Soviet Union, seeking support and legitimacy from these global powers. This foreign involvement not only shaped their political strategies and ideologies but also contributed to the rise and fall of these dictators.

Another important aspect to consider is the role of women during this time. While Latin American dictatorships were known for their patriarchal nature, women played a crucial role in the opposition movements and resistance against these regimes. Their experiences under dictatorships, including their participation in political activism and their struggles for gender equality, are essential to understanding the broader context of this era.

Furthermore, the economic policies and development under these dictatorships had a profound impact on the region. Many dictators implemented policies that favored the elite and multinational corporations, leading to widespread inequality and poverty. This economic disparity became a driving force behind the opposition movements and resistance against these dictators.

Additionally, the subchapter delves into the human rights violations and state repression that occurred under these dictatorships. Many individuals and groups who opposed the regimes faced imprisonment, torture, and even death. The ongoing struggles for justice sought to bring accountability for these human rights abuses and to bring closure for the victims and their families.

Cultural and artistic expressions also played a significant role during this era. Despite the restrictions imposed by the dictators, artists and intellectuals found ways to express dissent and critique the regimes through their work. These cultural expressions became a form of resistance and an outlet for the frustrations and aspirations of the population.

As historians, it is crucial to analyze and understand the legacy and long-term effects of these Latin American dictators on contemporary politics and society. By comparing different dictators and their methods of governance, we can gain insights into the similarities and differences in their approaches and their impact on the region.

In conclusion, the subchapter on socio-political changes and ongoing struggles for justice provides a comprehensive exploration of the multifaceted aspects of the era of Latin American dictators in the 1950s and 1960s. By examining the political strategies, economic policies, human rights violations, and cultural expressions of this period, historians can gain a deeper understanding of the complex dynamics and lasting effects of these dictators on Latin American society and politics.

Chapter 11: Comparative Analysis of Different Latin American Dictators and Their Methods of Governance in the 1950s and 1960s

Case study 1: Argentina under Juan Perón

Juan Perón's presidency in Argentina during the 1950s and 1960s provides a captivating case study for understanding the political strategies, economic policies, and social dynamics that characterized Latin American dictatorships at the time. Perón, a charismatic leader, implemented a distinct form of populism known as Peronism, which combined elements of nationalism, workers' rights, and social welfare programs. This subchapter delves into the various aspects of Perón's rule and its lasting impact on Argentine society.

One of the defining features of Perón's governance was his focus on economic development and industrialization. He introduced protectionist policies, nationalized key industries, and implemented labor reforms to improve the living conditions of Argentine workers. His policies resulted in significant economic growth, albeit with some drawbacks such as inflation and a growing public debt.

The study also explores the opposition movements and resistance faced by Perón's regime. While he enjoyed immense popularity among the working class, Perón's authoritarian tendencies and suppression of dissent sparked opposition from various sectors of society, including the military, the Catholic Church, and the middle class. The subchapter analyzes the strategies employed by these groups to challenge Perón's rule, including coup attempts and underground resistance organizations.

Furthermore, the subchapter addresses the human rights violations and state repression that occurred under Perón's regime. While Perón's populist policies initially aimed to uplift the working class, his government resorted to censorship, arbitrary arrests, and violence against political opponents. The subchapter examines the impact of these repressive measures on Argentine society and the long-term consequences for human rights in the country.

The chapter also explores the international relations and foreign involvement in Argentina during Perón's presidency. Perón's nationalist agenda, coupled with his anti-imperialist stance, led to strained relations with the United States. The subchapter analyzes the diplomatic challenges faced by Perón, as well as his efforts to align Argentina with other non-aligned countries and foster regional cooperation.

Finally, the subchapter concludes by examining the legacy and long-term effects of Perón's rule on contemporary Argentine politics and society. Peronism continues to be a significant force in Argentine politics, with successive governments adopting elements of Perón's ideology. The subchapter assesses the lasting impact of Perón's policies on Argentina's political landscape, social welfare system, and economic development.

By analyzing Argentina under Juan Perón, this subchapter contributes to a comprehensive understanding of the diverse strategies and ideologies employed by Latin American dictators during the 1950s and 1960s. It provides historians with valuable insights into the political, economic, and social dynamics of the era, facilitating comparative analysis with other Latin American dictators of the time.

Case study 2: Chile under Augusto Pinochet

Introduction:

This subchapter analyzes the rule of Augusto Pinochet, one of the most notorious Latin American dictators of the 1950s and 1960s. Pinochet's regime in Chile was marked by political repression, human rights violations, and economic reforms that had a lasting impact on the country. By examining Pinochet's strategies, ideologies, and their consequences, this case study sheds light on the complex dynamics of dictatorship in Latin America during this era.

Political Strategies and Ideologies:

Under Pinochet, Chile experienced a shift towards authoritarian rule, characterized by the dismantling of democratic institutions and the establishment of a military junta. Pinochet justified his actions as necessary to combat communism and restore order. His regime relied on tactics such as censorship, propaganda, and the persecution of political opponents to maintain control and suppress dissent.

Economic Policies and Development:

Pinochet's economic policies, known as the "Chicago Boys," aimed to transform Chile into a free-market economy. These policies included privatization, deregulation, and the reduction of state intervention. While these reforms led to economic growth and increased foreign investment, they also exacerbated income inequality and social disparities, leaving many Chileans marginalized and impoverished.

Human Rights Violations and State Repression:

Pinochet's regime was infamous for its widespread human rights abuses. Thousands of Chileans were victims of torture, forced disappearances, and extrajudicial killings. The military and secret police played a central role in carrying out these atrocities, targeting perceived enemies of the regime. The impact of state repression during this period continues to shape Chilean society and politics to this day.

Opposition Movements and Resistance:

Despite the regime's brutality, opposition movements emerged to challenge Pinochet's rule. Workers, students, and intellectuals organized protests, strikes, and underground resistance networks. The women's movement also played a significant role in resisting the dictatorship and advocating for human rights. These movements paved the way for Chile's eventual transition to democracy in the 1990s.

International Relations and Foreign Involvement:

Pinochet's regime received support from the United States and other Western powers during the Cold War. The U.S. saw Pinochet as a bulwark against communism and provided military aid and training to his forces. However, international pressure and condemnation grew as evidence of human rights abuses emerged, leading to Pinochet's arrest in 1998.

Legacy and Long-Term Effects:

Pinochet's dictatorship had a profound and lasting impact on Chilean society and politics. The scars of human rights abuses and state repression still resonate, and there remains a polarization between those who support Pinochet's economic reforms and those who condemn his authoritarian methods. The legacy of his regime continues to shape contemporary debates on justice, memory, and accountability in Chile.

Comparative Analysis:

By comparing Pinochet's rule with other Latin American dictators of the time, such as Fulgencio Batista in Cuba and Rafael Trujillo in the Dominican Republic, we can gain a deeper understanding of the different methods of governance employed during this era. This analysis highlights the complexities of autocratic rule and its impact on societies across the region.

Conclusion:

Augusto Pinochet's regime in Chile represents a dark chapter in Latin American history. The political repression, economic policies, and human rights violations under his rule continue to shape contemporary politics and society in Chile. Through a comparative analysis, we can gain valuable insights into the diverse strategies and legacies of Latin American dictators during the 1950s and 1960s.

Case study 3: Cuba under Fulgencio Batista

Fulgencio Batista was a prominent Latin American dictator who ruled over Cuba during the 1950s and early 1960s. His regime is an intriguing case study that offers valuable insights into the political strategies, economic policies, human rights violations, and international relations prevalent in Latin American dictatorships during this era.

Batista's rise to power began in 1952 when he staged a military coup, overthrowing the elected government of Carlos Prio Socarras. Once in power, Batista implemented a series of political strategies to consolidate his control. He suspended the constitution, dissolved political parties, and curtailed civil liberties, effectively suppressing opposition movements. However, his regime also faced significant challenges from various opposition groups, including student organizations and the revolutionary movement led by Fidel Castro.

Economically, Batista pursued policies that favored foreign investors and the elites, while neglecting the majority of the population. This led to growing inequality and widespread poverty, which fueled discontent and resistance against his rule. Additionally, his government was characterized by rampant corruption and cronyism, further exacerbating the economic disparities.

Under Batista's rule, Cuba also experienced severe human rights violations and state repression. The regime employed brutal methods to suppress dissent, including torture, disappearances, and extrajudicial killings. Opposition leaders, journalists, and intellectuals were often targeted, further stifling freedom of expression and dissent.

Batista's regime was deeply entrenched in the Cold War politics of the time. He maintained close ties with the United States, positioning Cuba as a strategic ally against the spread of communism in the region. This foreign involvement had far-reaching consequences, as it fueled popular resentment and contributed to the rise of revolutionary movements seeking to overthrow Batista, such as Castro's 26th of July Movement.

The legacy of Batista's rule continues to impact contemporary Cuban politics and society. The revolution led by Fidel Castro ultimately overthrew Batista in 1959, bringing about a radical transformation of the country's political, social, and economic landscape. The effects of Batista's regime, such as the economic disparities and human rights violations, continue to shape the challenges faced by Cuba today.

In conclusion, the case study of Cuba under Fulgencio Batista offers a comprehensive analysis of the political strategies, economic policies, human rights violations, and foreign involvement prevalent in Latin American dictatorships during the 1950s and 1960s. By examining this period, historians can gain valuable insights into the complex dynamics between dictators, opposition movements, and external actors, as well as the long-term effects of these regimes on contemporary politics and society.

Case study 4: Brazil under Getúlio Vargas

In this chapter, we delve into the fascinating era of Latin American dictators in the 1950s and 1960s, focusing specifically on Brazil under the rule of Getúlio Vargas. As historians, it is crucial to examine the political strategies, ideologies, and the impact of Cold War politics on the rise and fall of dictators in this period. Additionally, we explore the roles of women, economic policies, opposition movements, human rights violations, cultural expressions, international relations, and the long-term effects of this regime on contemporary society.

Getúlio Vargas, a charismatic and complex figure, ruled Brazil for two distinct periods, first from 1930 to 1945 and then again from 1951 until his death in 1954. His regime was marked by a unique blend of authoritarianism, populism, and nationalism. Vargas skillfully utilized political strategies such as censorship, propaganda, and repression to consolidate his power and maintain control over the Brazilian society.

Under Vargas' governance, Brazil experienced significant economic development and modernization. His administration implemented ambitious industrialization plans, which boosted the country's infrastructure, expanded the manufacturing sector, and created employment opportunities. These policies, known as import substitution industrialization, aimed to reduce dependence on foreign imports and stimulate domestic production.

However, Vargas' regime was not without its flaws and controversies. Opposition movements, such as the Communist Party and various labor unions, emerged to challenge his authoritarian rule. The government responded with repression, including the infamous "Estado Novo" period, characterized by censorship, political persecution, and human rights abuses.

Women played a significant but often overlooked role during this period. Vargas implemented labor laws that provided women with certain rights, including maternity leave and equal pay. However, these measures were often superficial, as women continued to face discrimination and limited opportunities for political participation.

The legacy of Vargas' regime is complex and continues to shape contemporary Brazilian politics and society. His populist discourse and policies laid the groundwork for future democratic movements, while also leaving behind a legacy of authoritarianism and repression. The long-term effects of Vargas' rule are still felt today, as Brazil grapples with issues of inequality, corruption, and political polarization.

By analyzing the case of Brazil under Getúlio Vargas, we gain valuable insights into the diverse methods of governance employed by different Latin American dictators in the 1950s and 1960s. This comparative analysis allows us to understand the complexities of this era and its lasting impacts on both the region and the world.

Case study 5: Haiti under Fancois Duvalier

Case Study 5: Haiti under Francois Duvalier

Francois Duvalier's reign in Haiti during the 1950s and 1960s provides a fascinating case study of a Latin American dictator and the impact of Cold War politics on his rise and fall. Duvalier, also known as "Papa Doc," came to power in 1957 and established one of the most brutal and repressive regimes in the region.

Duvalier's political strategy was grounded in a combination of populist appeals and state-sanctioned violence. He cultivated a personality cult, presenting himself as the savior of the Haitian people from the perceived threats of communism and external interference. Duvalier's ideology, known as "Duvalierism," blended elements of black nationalism, authoritarianism, and voodoo religious practices.

Under Duvalier's rule, Haiti experienced widespread human rights violations and state repression. His paramilitary force, the Tonton Macoutes, acted as a brutal instrument of control, carrying out extrajudicial killings, torture, and arbitrary arrests. Opposition movements and resistance against Duvalier were ruthlessly crushed, leading to a climate of fear and silence.

Women in Haiti also experienced unique challenges under Duvalier's dictatorship. While some women were co-opted into the regime's propaganda efforts, others faced sexual violence and exploitation. The regime sought to control women's bodies and reproductive rights, further entrenching gender inequality.

Economically, Duvalier implemented policies that benefited the ruling elite while neglecting the majority of the population. Corruption and embezzlement were rampant, exacerbating poverty and inequality. Despite promises of development, Haiti remained one of the poorest countries in the Western Hemisphere.

Internationally, Duvalier skillfully navigated the Cold War dynamics, playing on the fears of communism to secure support from the United States and other Western powers. However, his reliance on foreign aid and loans further deepened Haiti's economic dependence and hindered genuine progress.

The legacy of Duvalier's dictatorship continues to shape contemporary Haitian politics and society. The country struggles with the lingering effects of state repression, economic mismanagement, and political instability. The Duvalier regime serves as a cautionary tale of the dangers of unchecked power and the long-lasting consequences of authoritarian rule.

In comparing Duvalier's methods of governance with other Latin American dictators of the time, it becomes evident that while each regime had its unique characteristics, the underlying patterns of repression, human rights violations, and economic mismanagement were prevalent. Understanding these similarities and differences can shed light on the wider phenomenon of Latin American dictatorships in the 1950s and 1960s and how they shaped the region's political and social landscapes.

Case study 6: Republica Dominicana under Rafael Trujillo

Rafael Trujillo, often referred to as El Jefe, ruled the Dominican Republic with an iron fist from 1930 until his assassination in 1961. His regime provides an intriguing case study for historians interested in the political strategies, ideologies, and impact of Cold War politics on Latin American dictatorships during the 1950s and 1960s.

Trujillo's political strategy was centered on maintaining absolute control over the country. He established a cult of personality, relying on propaganda to cultivate an image of himself as the ultimate savior and protector of the Dominican people. Through his political party, the Partido Dominicano, he effectively eliminated any opposition and consolidated power within his own hands.

Ideologically, Trujillo employed a mix of authoritarianism, nationalism, and anti-communism. He promoted a strong sense of national identity and sought to control all aspects of Dominican society, from the economy to culture. Trujillo's regime was characterized by widespread human rights violations and state repression, with dissenters and opponents subjected to torture, imprisonment, and even assassination.

The impact of Cold War politics cannot be overlooked when analyzing Trujillo's rule. As the United States sought to combat the spread of communism in the region, they provided significant support to Trujillo's regime. This support bolstered his power and allowed him to suppress dissent with impunity. However, Trujillo's brutal methods ultimately led to his downfall as international pressure mounted and the United States withdrew its support.

Women in Trujillo's Dominican Republic experienced a highly gendered dictatorship. Trujillo sought to control and regulate women's bodies and behavior, imposing strict moral codes and promoting a traditional, subservient role for women in society. However, women also played a crucial role in the resistance against Trujillo, organizing and participating in opposition movements despite the risks they faced.

Economically, Trujillo pursued policies aimed at modernizing and expanding the Dominican economy. He attracted foreign investment and implemented infrastructure projects, but these gains were largely unevenly distributed, with a small elite benefiting at the expense of the majority. The legacy of Trujillo's economic policies continues to shape the Dominican Republic's development trajectory to this day.

In conclusion, the case of Republica Dominicana under Rafael Trujillo provides a rich and complex example of a Latin American dictator in the 1950s and 1960s. Trujillo's political strategies, ideologies, and the impact of Cold War politics, as well as the experiences of women, economic policies, and opposition movements all contribute to a comprehensive understanding of this era of Latin American history. By examining the legacy and long-term effects of Trujillo's rule, historians can gain valuable insights into the broader patterns and dynamics of Latin American dictatorships during this period.

Case study 7: Paraguay under Alfredo Stroessner

Alfredo Stroessner's reign as the dictator of Paraguay from 1954 to 1989 represents an important chapter in the history of Latin American dictators in the 1950s and 1960s. Stroessner's regime was marked by a combination of political strategies, human rights violations, economic policies, and international relations that shaped the country's trajectory during this period. This case study delves into the various aspects of Stroessner's rule and its impact on Paraguay.

Stroessner's rise to power can be attributed to his ability to exploit Cold War politics. He presented himself as a staunch anti-communist, aligning with the United States and receiving significant military and economic support. This support allowed Stroessner to consolidate his power and suppress opposition movements. However, this alliance also led to a disregard for human rights and widespread state repression. The Stroessner regime carried out numerous human rights violations, including forced disappearances, torture, and censorship, which resulted in the silencing of dissenting voices.

Economically, Stroessner implemented policies that aimed to promote development and industrialization. Paraguay experienced significant economic growth during his tenure, driven by agricultural exports and foreign investment. However, this growth was accompanied by widespread corruption and an increasing wealth gap. The benefits of economic development were not evenly distributed, leaving many Paraguayans marginalized and impoverished.

Opposition movements and resistance against Stroessner's rule were met with severe repression. Political parties were banned, and political opponents were persecuted, leading to a climate of fear and silence. Women, in particular, experienced heightened repression as they were subjected to sexual violence and discrimination. Despite these challenges, there were pockets of resistance, such as student movements and labor unions, that fought for democracy and social justice.

Culturally and artistically, the Stroessner era witnessed a stifling of creativity and expression. Artists and intellectuals faced censorship and were forced to either conform to the regime's ideology or face consequences. However, some artists found subtle ways to critique the regime through their work, contributing to the underground resistance movement.

Internationally, Stroessner maintained close ties with other Latin American dictators, participating in regional alliances such as Operation Condor. Paraguay became a safe haven for exiled members of other dictatorships, further entrenching its role in the region's political dynamics.

The legacy of Stroessner's rule continues to shape Paraguayan politics and society. The long-term effects are evident in the country's political institutions, economic inequalities, and social divisions. The study of Stroessner's regime provides valuable insights into the comparative analysis of different Latin American dictators and their methods of governance in the 1950s and 1960s, shedding light on the broader patterns and dynamics of autocratic rule in the region.

In conclusion, the case study of Paraguay under Alfredo Stroessner highlights the political strategies, human rights violations, economic policies, and international relations that characterized his dictatorship. The impact of his rule on Paraguay's political, economic, and social fabric continues to be felt today, making it a crucial case for historians studying the era of Latin American dictators in the 1950s and 1960s.

Case study 8: Nicaragua under Anastasio Somoza

Nicaragua, a small Central American country, experienced a tumultuous period under the rule of Anastasio Somoza in the 1950s and 1960s. Somoza, a member of the influential Somoza family, came to power following a coup against the democratically elected president, José María Moncada. This chapter will provide an in-depth analysis of Somoza's regime, exploring various aspects such as his political strategies, economic policies, human rights violations, and the impact of Cold War politics on his rule.

Anastasio Somoza's political strategies and ideologies played a crucial role in maintaining his grip on power. He established a highly centralized and authoritarian regime, suppressing opposition movements and silencing dissent through state repression. Somoza relied on a network of loyal military officials and intelligence agencies to eliminate any threats to his rule. His regime was characterized by corruption, nepotism, and favoritism, as the Somoza family amassed immense wealth and controlled key sectors of the Nicaraguan economy.

Economically, Somoza implemented policies that favored foreign investors and multinational corporations, leading to the exploitation of Nicaragua's resources and widening economic inequalities. While some sectors experienced growth, the majority of the population remained impoverished and marginalized. Somoza's economic policies further exacerbated social tensions and contributed to the rise of opposition movements demanding social justice and equality.

The Somoza regime was notorious for its human rights violations and state repression. Dissidents, activists, and political opponents faced arbitrary arrests, torture, and extrajudicial killings. Women, in particular, experienced gender-based violence and discrimination under Somoza's rule. Despite these atrocities, opposition movements and resistance against the regime emerged, with students, workers, and peasants organizing protests and strikes.

Cold War politics greatly influenced Somoza's rule, as he capitalized on the United States' fear of communism to secure military and economic support. The United States saw Somoza as a reliable ally in the region and turned a blind eye to his authoritarian practices. However, this support eventually waned as international pressure mounted, and the Somoza regime was seen as a hindrance to democratic progress in Nicaragua.

The legacy of Anastasio Somoza and his authoritarian rule continues to shape contemporary Nicaraguan politics and society. The country still grapples with issues of inequality, corruption, and political instability, highlighting the long-term effects of Somoza's governance. Comparative analysis of different Latin American dictators in the 1950s and 1960s reveals similarities in their methods of governance, underscoring the need for a comprehensive understanding of this era in Latin American history.

In conclusion, the case study of Nicaragua under Anastasio Somoza provides valuable insights into the political strategies, economic policies, human rights violations, and foreign involvement during the era of Latin American dictators in the 1950s and 1960s. Understanding the complexities of Somoza's regime and its impact on contemporary society is crucial for historians studying the age of Latin American dictators.

Case study 9: Peru under Manuel Odria

Introduction:

In this chapter, we will delve into the case study of Peru under the rule of Manuel Odria during the 1950s and 1960s. Odria's dictatorship provides a fascinating lens through which to analyze the political strategies, economic policies, human rights violations, and opposition movements that characterized Latin American dictatorships during this period.

Political Strategies and Ideologies:

Manuel Odria rose to power through a military coup in 1948, establishing an authoritarian regime in Peru. His government emphasized nationalism and populism, promoting policies that aimed to improve the living conditions of the working class. However, Odria's regime was also marked by repression, censorship, and the suppression of political opposition.

Impact of Cold War Politics:

During the Cold War era, Latin American dictators often aligned themselves with either the United States or the Soviet Union. Odria leaned towards the United States, receiving economic and military assistance in exchange for his support in the fight against communism. This foreign involvement shaped both the policies and the longevity of his regime.

Women's Roles and Experiences:

Under Odria's dictatorship, women faced limited opportunities for political participation and suffered from gender-based discrimination. However, some women actively resisted the regime and played significant roles in opposition movements, challenging societal norms and advocating for women's rights.

Economic Policies and Development:

Odria implemented protectionist economic policies, focusing on industrialization and infrastructure development. This approach aimed to strengthen the national economy and reduce dependency on foreign imports. While these policies brought some economic growth, they also contributed to income inequality and marginalized rural populations.

Opposition Movements and Resistance:

Odria faced opposition from various groups, including left-wing parties, intellectuals, and students. These movements organized protests, strikes, and acts of civil disobedience, challenging the regime's authoritarian rule and demanding political reform.

Human Rights Violations and State Repression:

Throughout Odria's regime, human rights violations were widespread, including arbitrary arrests, torture, and extrajudicial killings. State repression targeted political opponents, labor activists, and indigenous communities, leading to a climate of fear and silence.

Cultural and Artistic Expressions:

Despite censorship and repression, cultural and artistic expressions thrived during Odria's regime. Artists and writers used their work to critique the dictatorship and express dissent, creating a vibrant underground scene that challenged the regime's control over public discourse.

International Relations and Foreign Involvement:

Odria maintained close ties with the United States, receiving economic and military aid. He also sought to strengthen regional alliances, particularly within Latin America, as a way to counterbalance Soviet influence in the region.

Legacy and Long-Term Effects:

The legacy of Odria's dictatorship continues to shape Peruvian politics and society. The authoritarian practices and human rights abuses of his regime left a lasting impact, prompting subsequent governments to address historical injustices and promote democratic reforms.

Comparative Analysis:

By analyzing Peru under Odria alongside other Latin American dictators of the time, we can gain a comprehensive understanding of the diverse methods of governance employed in the region. This comparative analysis allows us to identify common patterns, differences in ideologies, and the impact of external factors on the rise and fall of Latin American dictatorships in the 1950s and 1960s.

Conclusion:

The case study of Peru under Manuel Odria offers valuable insights into the complexities of Latin American dictatorships during the 1950s and 1960s. Understanding the political strategies, economic policies, resistance movements, and human rights violations of this period is crucial for historians studying the age of Latin American dictators and its long-term effects on contemporary politics and society.

Case study 10: Cuba under Fidel Castro

Fidel Castro's rule in Cuba from the late 1950s to the early 2000s is an intriguing and complex chapter in the history of Latin American dictators. Castro's rise to power was marked by his charismatic leadership and his promise to bring social justice and equality to the Cuban people. This case study delves into the various aspects of Castro's regime, examining its political strategies, impact on the Cold War politics, economic policies, human rights violations, and legacy.

Under Castro's leadership, Cuba experienced a radical shift in its political ideology and governance. He established a socialist state, implementing policies aimed at redistributing wealth and nationalizing industries. His regime also emphasized education and healthcare, leading to significant improvements in these areas. However, critics argue that these achievements came at the cost of political freedoms and human rights, as dissent was suppressed through state repression and censorship.

The Cold War politics had a profound influence on Castro's rule. In 1961, the failed Bay of Pigs invasion by the United States solidified Castro's position as a leader opposing American imperialism. Cuba became a key player in the Cold War, aligning itself with the Soviet Union and receiving economic and military support. This alliance heightened tensions with the United States, leading to the Cuban Missile Crisis in 1962.

The economic policies pursued by Castro's regime had mixed results. While Cuba made significant progress in areas such as healthcare and literacy, its centrally planned economy struggled to meet the demands of the population. The Cuban people faced shortages of basic necessities, and the economy became heavily dependent on subsidies from the Soviet Union.

Opposition movements and resistance against Castro's regime were met with severe repression. Political dissent was systematically suppressed, with many dissidents being imprisoned or forced into exile. Women's roles and experiences under Castro's rule were also shaped by state policies, which sought to increase gender equality but often fell short in practice.

Cultural and artistic expressions during Castro's era were closely monitored and controlled by the state. Artists and intellectuals faced censorship and were expected to adhere to the principles of the revolution. However, despite these restrictions, Cuban culture continued to thrive and produce internationally acclaimed artists.

The legacy and long-term effects of Castro's rule continue to shape contemporary Cuban politics and society. Despite his death in 2016, Castro's influence remains significant, and Cuba faces ongoing challenges in transitioning to a more open and democratic system.

Comparative analysis of different Latin American dictators in the 1950s and 1960s reveals the unique strategies and methods of governance employed by Castro. His regime differed from other dictatorships in the region, particularly in its socialist ideology and alignment with the Soviet Union. Understanding these differences provides valuable insights into the diverse political landscape of Latin America during this era.

Overall, the case study on Cuba under Fidel Castro offers historians a comprehensive analysis of the political, economic, social, and cultural dimensions of his rule. It sheds light on the complexities and contradictions of his regime, contributing to a better understanding of the broader history of Latin American dictators in the 1950s and 1960s.

Conclusion: Insights and Reflections on Comparative Autocrats in Latin America's 1950s and 1960s

As we come to the end of our exploration into the world of Latin American dictators in the 1950s and 1960s, it is important to reflect on the insights gained and the impact these autocrats had on the region.

Throughout this book, we have delved into various aspects of their rule, from political strategies and ideologies to human rights violations and state repression. We have also examined the influence of Cold War politics, women's roles, economic policies, opposition movements, cultural expressions, and international relations on these dictatorships. By comparing different Latin American dictators and their methods of governance, we have gained a comprehensive understanding of this tumultuous era.

One of the key insights we have gained is the diverse political strategies and ideologies employed by these autocrats. From the populist rhetoric of Perón in Argentina to the militaristic rule of Pinochet in Chile, each dictator had their own unique approach to maintaining power. This diversity highlights the complex nature of Latin American politics during this time and challenges the notion of a monolithic dictatorship.

Furthermore, the impact of Cold War politics cannot be understated. The United States and the Soviet Union played significant roles in shaping the rise and fall of these dictators. While some leaders aligned themselves with the United States in their fight against communism, others sought support from the Soviet Union or adopted a non-aligned stance. This geopolitical context greatly influenced the trajectory of these regimes and the level of foreign involvement they experienced.

Another important aspect that emerged from our analysis is the resistance and opposition movements that emerged against these dictators. From student protests to guerrilla warfare, various groups challenged the authoritarian rule and fought for democracy and human rights. These movements not only highlight the resilience of the Latin American people but also their desire for a better future.

The legacy of these autocrats continues to shape contemporary politics and society in Latin America. The long-term effects of their rule can still be felt in terms of economic disparities, social inequality, and political instability. Understanding this legacy is crucial for addressing these challenges and building a more inclusive and democratic future.

In conclusion, our exploration of Latin American dictators in the 1950s and 1960s has provided valuable insights into the complexities of this era. By examining their political strategies, ideologies, impact on human rights, and the resistance they faced, we have gained a comprehensive understanding of this turbulent period. It is our hope that this study will contribute to a deeper understanding of Latin American history and serve as a reminder of the importance of democracy and human rights in shaping a just society.

www.ingramcontent.com/pod-product-compliance
Lightning Source LLC
Chambersburg PA
CBHW031501130726
47989CB00003B/1498